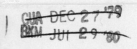

Lerner Wildlife Library

Animals of the MOUNTAINS

written by Sylvia A. Johnson
illustrated by Alcuin C. Dornisch

 Lerner Publications Company
Minneapolis, Minnesota

LIBRARY OF CONGRESS CATALOGING IN PUBLICATION DATA

Johnson, Sylvia A.
    Animals of the mountains.

    (Lerner Wildlife Library)
    SUMMARY: Brief descriptions of the characteristics and
behavior of ten mountain animals—the American pika, Himalayan ibex, chamois, vicuña, giant panda, mountain gorilla,
snow leopard, mountain goat, bighorn sheep, and grizzly bear.

    1. Alpine fauna—Juvenile literature. [1. Alpine animals.
2. Animals—Habits and behavior] I. Dornisch, Alcuin C.
II. Title.

QL113.J6 1976   599'.09'0943   75-27756
ISBN 0-8225-1277-7

Copyright © 1976 by Lerner Publications Company

Published simultaneously in Canada by
J. M. Dent & Sons (Canada) Ltd., Don Mills, Ontario

Manufactured in the United States of America

International Standard Book Number: 0-8225-1277-7
Library of Congress Catalog Card Number: 75-27756

Contents

Animals of the MOUNTAINS

Rising up from the face of the earth in jagged peaks or in gentle swells, the world's mountains form a fascinating and unique environment. Around their heights swirl clouds of mist or snow, while at their feet stretch green forests and fertile plains. On their slopes live plants and animals unknown to the inhabitants of the flatlands —living things whose characteristics have been shaped by this harsh natural environment.

The mountain environment is harsh because mountains are what they are: masses of land that project high above the surface of the earth. Although the actual height of the world's mountains varies from the towering peaks of the Himalayas in Asia to the rounded hills of North America's Appalachian range, all mountains are higher than the land surrounding them. And height is always accompanied by cold. The air on the mountain tops is colder than the air at lower levels because it is drier and thus less able to hold the warming infrared rays of the sun. Because of this difference in temperature, the climate on a mountain changes vertically, becoming colder with every foot or meter of height.

This pattern of temperature change is typical of all mountains, whether they are located in tropical areas near the Equator or in cold arctic regions. Of course, the climate of a mountain is also affected by the climate of the surrounding area, so that tropical mountains generally have milder overall climates than mountains in colder regions. Nevertheless, the contrasting zones of life that are created by temperature changes can be found on any mountain, regardless of its location.

The effects of temperature changes can be seen most clearly in mountain plants. Plants that are able to grow on the lower slopes of a mountain usually cannot survive at higher levels. Vegetation on the lower slopes may grow tall and straight, but higher up, it falls victim to the mountain's cold temperatures and harsh winds. Plants native to the mountain heights must grow close to the ground in order to conserve heat and to escape bitter mountain winds. These plants are usually small, with tiny leaves and blossoms that do not require large amounts of energy for growth. They often have large and complicated root systems that enable them to find adequate moisture in the thin soil and to cling to steep mountain slopes.

Trees growing on mountain slopes become smaller and less numerous the higher up the mountain they are found. As they approach the *timberline*, the point beyond which trees cannot grow, they become stunted and distorted, bent by the wind into fantastic shapes or clinging to the ground like shrubs. Beyond the timberline is the region of *alpine tundra*, a barren zone where only the smallest, sturdiest plants can survive. And beyond the tundra, at the very top of the highest mountains, there is only rock and snow and ice.

The animals that live in the mountains are not quite so much at the mercy of the strenuous mountain environment as are the plants, since they are able to move from place to place and thus avoid the very worst conditions. Nevertheless, mountain animals must make their homes on the steep and rocky slopes, and they must get their food from the often scarce resources available to them. And mountain animals must have ways of protecting themselves from extremes of cold and from the wind's piercing blasts.

Mountain creatures possess many characteristics that enable them to survive and even thrive in their difficult environment. Some members of the goat and sheep families, for instance, have become specialists in mountain climbing, making good use of their uniquely constructed hooves in clinging to steep slopes or walking along narrow ledges. These *herbivores*, or plant eaters, are also skilled

Mountainous Regions of the World

in getting as much nourishment as possible by grazing continuously on the sparse mountain vegetation. Some mountain animals must depend on their hunting skills for food; these are the *carnivores*, the flesh eaters that prey on the elusive inhabitants of the mountain heights. Carnivore and herbivore alike are prey to the cold temperatures of the mountains. But flesh eaters like the snow leopard and plant eaters like the mountain goat are protected from the severe cold of mountain winters by heavy coats of fur or hair. Other mountain animals hibernate to avoid winter cold or migrate to the lower, warmer mountain slopes.

The inhabitants of the mountains vary in their habits and their ways of life, but all have learned to make the most out of their difficult environment. In the following pages, you will have an opportunity to meet a few of these fascinating and resourceful mountain creatures.

American Pika

When winter wind and snow sweep the mountain ranges of North America, many small animals retreat into the safety of their dens. Here they enter the state of deep sleep known as *hibernation*. Hibernating animals do not need food—they live off the fat stored in their bodies. But the small mountain animal called the pika (PIE-kuh) must have a supply of winter food because it spends the cold season wide awake. This furry little relative of the rabbit begins preparing for winter while the summer sun is still warm on the mountain slopes. It spends long summer days cutting down grasses and plants with its sharp teeth and carrying them back to its den among the rocks. Before storing the plants away, the pika spreads them out so that they will dry in the sun. If rain begins to fall, the little animal will quickly move its haystack in under the rocks to keep it from getting wet. After the hay has completely dried, it is stored away in the pika's underground home, ready for winter. When the energetic pikas are not busy gathering food or taking care of their haystacks, they like to sit out in the open air and enjoy the warmth of the sun. If danger threatens, one pika will give a high-pitched squeal, and every pika within hearing distance will scurry under the protection of the rocks.

Himalayan Ibex

Many mountain animals wear splendid sets of horns on their heads, but the horns of the Himalayan ibex (EYE-beks) are among the most impressive of all. Large and ridged, they sweep back from the animal's head in graceful curves that turn forward at the ends. The horns of an adult male ibex may be as much as 60 inches (150 centimeters) in length. The female's horns are much shorter, as is common among many types of horned mountain animals. Ibexes are members of the wild goat family (genus *Capra*), and they make their homes in various mountain ranges scattered throughout Europe, Asia, and Africa. In addition to the Himalayan ibex, there is an Alpine ibex, a species that lives in the Pyrenees Mountains in Spain, and another whose home is in the cold mountains of Siberia. All the species of ibexes, of course, are skilled at climbing and leaping among the rocks and cliffs of their rugged environments. Even young ibexes are expert mountaineers. Within minutes after birth, they are able to follow their mothers as they climb steep slopes or bound over rocky hillsides.

Rocky Mountain Goat

A spot of white on a distant mountain slope, a shaggy form outlined against the sky—this is all that most human observers ever see of the Rocky Mountain goat (*Oreamnos americanus*). This remarkable animal makes its home on the mountain heights high above the timberline. Amid the rocky crags and steep slopes of this dangerous environment, the Rocky Mountain goat is perfectly at ease. It walks calmly along narrow ledges overlooking deep canyons and moves quickly over hillsides that might seem straight up and down to the human eye. Like the bighorn sheep, an animal that inhabits the lower mountain slopes, the Rocky Mountain goat has hooves especially designed for mountain climbing. In the center of the divided hoof is a spongy pad that enables the animal to cling to narrow ledges or rocky hillsides without slipping. The hooves of the Rocky Mountain goat are shiny black, as are its short, and very sharp, horns. The animal's dazzling white coat is made up of an outer layer of long hair and an inner layer of thick wool—warm protection against cold mountain winds. Both male and female Rocky Mountain goats have beards, like the familiar domestic goat. Despite the animal's name and its close resemblance to the domestic goat, however, the Rocky Mountain goat is more closely related to the antelope family than to the goat family. In fact, it is often referred to as a "goat-antelope." Another mountain dweller, the chamois of the European Alps, is also a member of this unusual group of animals.

Giant Panda

The giant panda (*Ailuropoda melanoleuca*) is a familiar and well-loved animal, but it is also a mysterious one. Throughout the world, people flock to zoos to admire captive pandas, but few people have seen the giant panda in its natural surroundings. This is because the animal comes from a very remote part of the world—a mountainous region located in southwestern China and eastern Tibet. The panda's home is a land of high peaks and thick bamboo forests, a land swept by cold wind and rain. Hidden in the mists and clouds of the mountains, the giant panda seems to spend most of its time eating. Since the panda is a large animal, it must eat a great deal to supply the energy that it needs. Its favorite food is bamboo—the leaves, the shoots, and even the woody stems of this unusual plant. When munching on bamboo, the panda sits up straight, with its hind legs stretched out in front of it. The animal uses its front paws to hold the plant up to its mouth. It is able to grasp the pieces of bamboo by using what scientists call its extra thumb—a flesh-covered knob of bone located on the bottom of its front paws. By holding the plant stems between this "thumb" and its five fingers, or claws, the giant panda can get a good grip on its leafy food.

Vicuña

Although we usually think of camels as creatures of the flat, sandy desert, several members of the camel family actually make their homes in the mountainous regions of South America. The familiar llama is a South American camel that has been tamed by humans. Another member of the camel family, the graceful little vicuña (vih-KOON-yuh), roams wild over the high plateaus of the Andes Mountains in Peru,

Bolivia, and Chile. The vicuñas' home is a land of windy, rolling plains, about 12,000 feet (3,600 meters) above sea level. The sparse grass that grows in this dry country supplies the animals with all the food they need. Vicuñas are used to the harshness of their environment and can survive very well if they are left in peace. But today, these unusual mountain animals have become quite rare. They are being hunted and killed in large numbers by people who want to use their fleece to make cloth. The vicuña has long been famous for the softness and fineness of its fleece. Centuries ago, in the days when the Incas ruled Peru, only members of the royal family were allowed to wear clothing made out of vicuña fleece. Once every four years, the Inca rulers would send hunters out to kill the vicuñas and to bring in their skins. At no other time could the animals be hunted. Today, the government of modern Peru has also made strict laws regulating the hunting of vicuñas, in an effort to protect these inhabitants of the mountains from extinction.

18 Chamois

The graceful chamois (SHAM-ih) is another mountain animal that belongs to the family of goat-antelopes. But unlike its North American relative the Rocky Mountain goat, the chamois looks more like the antelope side of the family than the goat side. At home in the high mountains of Europe and Asia, the chamois is as sure-footed as all the other hooved mammals that inhabit the world's mountain ranges. It can make leaps of 20 feet (6 meters) or more and land lightly on its slender front legs, without a jar or a shock. The chamois is also known for its keen eyesight and hearing. No wonder that hunters have a difficult time catching up with this mountain creature in its home territory. Nevertheless, people do hunt chamois for their flesh and for their hides, out of which is made the soft, flexible leather called *chamois skin*. A few chamois are caught by hunters, but most escape to continue their peaceful lives among the rocks and crags of the mountain tops.

Snow Leopard

One of the most beautiful of the mountain animals is the snow leopard, sometimes called the ounce (*Uncia uncia*). This big cat lives only in the high mountains of Central Asia, at altitudes above 5,000 feet (1,500 meters). The snow leopard looks quite different from the animal that we usually think of as the leopard—the sleek cat that inhabits tropical Africa and Asia. Because the snow leopard lives in a cold climate, its fur is not sleek but thick and long, as much as three inches (about 7.5 centimeters) in length on the underside of its body. The tropical leopard and most other big cats have fairly large ears in proportion to the size of their heads, but the ears of the snow leopard are small. This difference, too, is the result of the snow leopard's adaptation to a cold environment. Small ears are not as much affected by cold as large ears because they allow less body heat to escape. Knowing this, we would expect that all the extended parts of the snow leopard's body would be small, but this is not the case. The animal's fur-covered tail is at least three feet (90 centimeters) long. Although the length of this magnificent tail might seem impractical, it does serve some useful purposes. When the snow leopard curls up to sleep, it uses its long tail to cover the tip of its nose, shielding it from cold winds. Even more important, the huge tail helps the animal to keep its balance when it is engaged in the delicate art of hunting. Like all big cats, the snow leopard is a *predator*—an animal that lives by killing and eating other animals. Stealing quietly up to a grazing deer or mountain sheep, the snow leopard leaps on its prey with a powerful bound. The grass-eating animal provides a meal for the meat-eating cat, and one more link in the chain of natural life is formed.

Mountain Gorilla

Gorilla! Just mention the word, and most people tremble with fear. Everyone knows that gorillas are fierce and dangerous animals, that they attack humans whenever they get the chance. The *fact* is that gorillas are gentle, peaceful creatures who rarely attack any living thing. During the last 20 years, scientists have been learning the truth about gorillas by studying the huge animals in their natural surroundings. The gorilla's home is the rain forest of central Africa. The lowland gorilla lives in the western part of the continent, while the rare mountain gorilla can be found only on the forested slopes of certain

mountain ranges in east central Africa. Mountain gorillas live in groups made up of anywhere from 3 to 30 members. The leader of the gorilla troop is an adult male, who can be recognized by the silver-white hair covering his back. Also in the troop are several black-backed males—younger gorillas whose hair has not yet turned white. Female gorillas and their young— infants, toddlers, and teenagers—make up the rest of the gorilla troop.

Mountain gorillas spend much of their time wandering through the forest in search of food. The animals eat all kinds of plants— wild celery, bamboo, nettles—and they eat a great deal during the long hours of the day. Around dusk, the gorilla troop is ready to settle down for the night. In preparation for sleep, each animal makes itself a nest, either on the ground or in the low branches of a tree. (Young gorillas share their mothers' nests until they are several years old.) An hour or so after the sun rises, the gorillas leave their beds and set off on their daily ramble through the rain forest.

Bighorn Sheep

High on the slopes of the Rocky Mountains and other North American mountain ranges lives the bighorn sheep (*Ovis canadensis*), an animal very much at home in the mountain environment. This distant relative of the domestic sheep is a fearless mountain climber who can scramble up and down steep slopes with great ease. When fleeing from danger or running just for the fun of it, bighorn sheep move quickly and gracefully. Their divided hooves enable them to keep their balance on narrow ledges, and their sturdy bodies absorb the shock of long leaps and hard landings. Throughout the year, bighorn sheep climb over the mountain slopes, searching for the grasses and plants that make up their diet. When winter comes to the mountains, the sheep must often dig for their food beneath a blanket of snow. Winter is a harsh season on the mountain heights. For the bighorn sheep, early winter is also the season for mating, the time when new life has its beginning. During this period, the mature male sheep, called *rams*, fight each other over the possession of the female sheep, or *ewes*. The rams use their enormous horns as weapons during these battles, clashing them together in head-to-head combat. The winner of the violent contest gets the pick of the ewes as mates, but even the loser is allowed to play a part in the mating activities. About five months later, when the spring wildflowers are in bloom, the bighorn lambs are born, usually one to each ewe. A few hours after birth, the lambs are running and leaping over the mountainside almost as fearlessly as their parents.

Grizzly Bear

The grizzly bear (*Ursus horribilis*) is probably the most famous member of the bear family. At one time, this huge animal lived throughout a large part of western North America, but now it can be found only in a few isolated mountain regions. Grizzlies have retreated to the mountains in order to get away from human beings, with their guns and their ever-expanding civilization. In spite of the fact that there are not many grizzly bears left, the animal's reputation for fierceness remains as strong as ever. The grizzly *is* a frightening-looking creature, with its large head, heavy body, and long, straight claws. But recent studies have shown that grizzlies do not seem to be naturally aggressive—they usually attack only in self-defense. Of course, the grizzly, like all bears, won't allow anyone or anything to get in its way when it is looking for something to eat. The grizzly's menu is similar to that of most other North American bears. It consists of nuts, berries, and plants of all kinds, small mammals such as field mice and ground squirrels, and larger mammals like porcupines and domestic sheep. Grizzlies are also very fond of fish, like so many of their relatives. Wading into the shallow waters of a salmon or trout stream, a grizzly will wait patiently until a fish swims by. The big bear pounces on the fish, pinning it down with one paw and then taking it in its teeth. After enjoying its fish dinner on shore, the grizzly wades back into the stream for another catch.

Scale of Animal Sizes

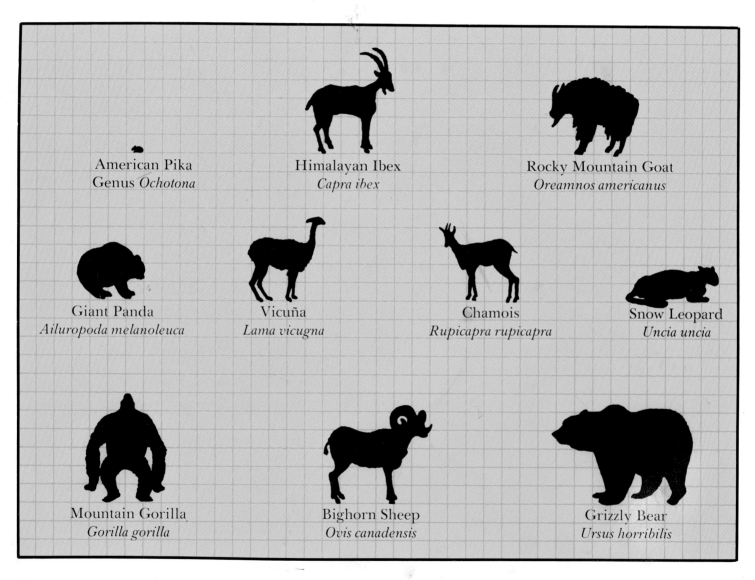

American Pika
Genus *Ochotona*

Himalayan Ibex
Capra ibex

Rocky Mountain Goat
Oreamnos americanus

Giant Panda
Ailuropoda melanoleuca

Vicuña
Lama vicugna

Chamois
Rupicapra rupicapra

Snow Leopard
Uncia uncia

Mountain Gorilla
Gorilla gorilla

Bighorn Sheep
Ovis canadensis

Grizzly Bear
Ursus horribilis

= 1 Foot   = 1 Meter   *Animals of the Mountains*